STÉPHANIE M

Autism
Why My Son

"Autism Why My Son"
© 2021 by **Stéphanie Maty**
ISBN United Kingdom: 9781800498594

Published by
La Maison du Livre
London, United Kingdom

Contact Info
La Maison du Livre
23 Felton Walk
Newcastle Upon Tyne,
NE6 2EW

UK: +44 (0) 191 276 1669
www.lamaisondulivre.store
Email: publietonlivre@lamaisondulivre.store

All biblical quotations come from the New King James Version of the Bible, unless otherwise indicated.

All reproduction, production and translation rights reserved.

First edition in English 2021
Original title "Autism Why My Son"

This book is the property of the charity **"Steph Together"**, therefore all sales will be donated to the charity

Contents

I.	Forewords 11
II.	Acknowledgements 15
III.	Dedication 19

Chapter I   Life and its surprises 21

Chapter II   Never two without three 33

Chapter III   The diagnosis 43

Chapter IV   The impact in my family 55

Chapter V   Acceptance and Compliance 69

Chapter VI   New momentum 79

IV.   Conclusion 91

Foreword

As a teenager, **Stephanie Maty** experienced a family tragedy that changed her perception of life forever. This child, who lived in a Catholic parental circle, lost her mother at an age when everyone needs a mother the most.

Several years later, she decided to go to England to seek a better future. She left behind her father, her four brothers and her first child, Marie. After several years, **Marie** joined her in this foreign land.

Stephanie, who was already a mother and had gone through pregnancy several times, experienced one of her pregnancies she had the grace to carry in a special way. During this phase, which she describes as «never experienced before», her partner revealed the best version of himself, making these nine months of pregnancy a moment of immense joy that plunged her into an atmosphere of happiness.

Stéphane, her only son, who was affectionately called *«Happy Boy»* by his father, will come into the world with *«a disease»*. Before the birth of her son, the author had no knowledge of the handicap that is **autism.**

Terrified that her child would not be liked the others, this mother first called in health specialists who, after thorough examinations, defined what she thought would be cured with time as **«a condition»**...

«AUTISM: WHY MY SON?» is an autobiography that tells the story of the author's journey to better accompany her son to his mental evolution. From the negative impact that her son's condition had on her family to the rejection she faced, we read how this mother struggled to better lead her son.

Acknowledgements

To Apostle Wilfried Rozogue for his big heart, his patience and his unconditional support in bringing this book to life.

To **La Maison du livre Ltd** and all its team for your patience and encouragement in the writing of this book.

To my children **Marie, Jennifer, Stéphane**, and last but not least to my youngest daughter **Elizabeth, ELIZA Mat.** I bless the Lord for your life and especially for all the efforts you keep making to help your brother Stephane become Independent. You do not hesitate to defend him in complex situations because you understand his condition. Thank you my young Lioness.

To my grandchildren who have always believed in me and never stopped supporting me.

To my brothers **Blaise, Romain, Constantin Didier** and **Eti**; the love that binds us is unconditional. You have always been there for me. Thank you.

To all the members of **Christ Victory Church International**, especially to **General Overseas** Pastor **Osman Gyasi-Mensah** for all the prayers. You never had enough of me.

Thank you **M Hendou** for being present in the lives of your loved ones.

To the Bible study group, **People of God**, for your trust in me, thank you.

To the great **Mankang** and **Bale** family for your support.

To my brother from another mother **Mr. Mbala**, who has always supported me through all the trials of my life.

To **Victoire Essien** (Mami-ma), who has always believed in me. Thank you for your precious advice, woman of God.

I would also like to thank all those people who have supported me from near and far.

A Special Mention
I would especially like to thank my daughter **Jennifer Maty** for her big heart, the patience and the Love that you keep showing to your brothers and sisters as well as to your parents.

Jennifer, you have always been there when everyone has left. I bless the Lord for your sense of maturity. Please don't ever change your heart.

Dedication

I want to dedicate this book to all the mothers of the world, especially those who have children who are different, children with ADHD, Dyspraxia, Dyslexia, Autism, Aspergers

Or any learning difficulty Autism, Asperger's, ADHD, Dyspraxia, Dyslexia or any learning difficulty   Disabilities...

To those mothers in desperate situations,

May our fears diminish so that our hopes Increase.

Chapter 1
« Life and its surprises »

«When innocence is part of us, we see life as a paradise where the people we love remain eternal. Unfortunately, when this perspective is interrupted, we find ourselves in a kind of osmosis that allows us to embark on adventures that should not have engulfed us anytime soon. »

My name is **Stéphanie Maty**, I was born in **Cameroon** in the town of **Nkongsamba** in the plain of **Mbo**. Because of its very high mountain content, this city is commonly called the **city of mountains**...

According to my mother, I was born prematurely, not in a hospital, not in a house, but by the river. My mother told me that she went there to do her chores. That day she was there to do the laundry. Suddenly, a heavy rain came. While she was preparing to go home, I was also preparing to leave the place that had been my world for a long time. She thought the rain was a sign that I was coming...

I lost my mother when I was thirteen years old. As the eldest of a family of five children, of which I am the only daughter, my life was very confused after my mother's departure because there was no longer anyone I could take as a reference. I didn't understand how you could lose your mother at that age. Life seemed very cruel to me and I blamed the whole world. My mother and I had never been separated while she was alive, I was with her everywhere and at all times. During the holidays at the end of the school year, I refused to go to uncles' or aunts' houses because I preferred to be with this woman whom I loved deeply. Sometimes I wondered why it was my mother who had left and not someone else. Before she died, my mother had given me the responsibility of looking after my brothers; **Blaise, Romain, Constantin,** and **Didier** who was the youngest. **Didier** was only nine months old when the tragedy occurred. I still remember the day when she said to me with a defeated but still smiling face: «My daughter, promise me that you will always take care of your little brothers if anything happens to me. «I answered her with an encouraging voice: *«Mom, nothing bad will happen to you, and soon everything will be fine, you will be healthy again and we will all be happy again! »*. I don't think I realised the seriousness of what was happening before my eyes.

From the announcement of my mother's death to her funeral, the atmosphere was unbearable. I felt like I was half breathing, as if I had left this world with her, I walked without feeling any sensation. Even the air on my skin had no effect. Everything was gloomy and our house, where we once lived in perfect harmony with a mother whose ability to manage her home I admired, was now a place of intense sadness. Each of us tried as best we could to get through this difficult time by doing what we felt was right. I can see Dad sitting and staring at the seat where Mom was sitting. Very often tears would flow from his eyes and so that he wouldn't know that I was affected by seeing him like this, I would go back to my room and cry, because it was the first time my father was so distressed... No sooner did I understand the importance of having a mother than when I lost mine and was forced to become one by circumstance.

While I was going through one of the darkest moments of my life, my story spread throughout the neighbourhood and everyone in turn tried to comfort me. This is how I met **Michel**. Our exchanges were, at first, friendly. He supported me emotionally in the situation I was going through. I found in him a friend, a confidant, a shoulder to cry on. Being in the same school, we walked together when we went to school. We became accomplices, and got used to seeing each other.

One day **Michel** told me that he wanted us to meet in the evening. I was hesitant because I was afraid of what might happen. But after his insistence, I agreed to meet him at **«Camp Bertaud»**. I was use to going to church every Sunday evening, so it was easy for me to leave the family

Life and its surprises

home without being questioned about where I was going. When I arrived at our meeting place, I saw Michael already there waiting for me. It was amazing how his words could soothe my aching heart. And in the darkness of the night, we were getting closer to each other. This friendship, which at first was platonic, turned into a romance that plunged me into a new experience. But as an innocent girl, I did not understand that a being who would become my first child was now germinating within me.

One day, as I entered the kitchen of *mama* **'Ndongo**, who was skilfully pounding the cassava leaves that would be used to prepare the meal, I noticed that she was quite different from the other times I had visited her. She wasn't looking me in the eye as usual, but her gaze was directed at my stomach and the closer I got to her, the more her gaze was directed at my neck. It was as if she was counting every beat of my heart. My mother's friend was very quiet compared to the other times. After several strokes of the pestle in her mortar, she would stop and stare at me for a long time before resuming her chore. Several minutes of silence later, she asked me: «*How do you feel*, **Dédé** (my pet name)?» I answered with the most beautiful smile: «*I'm fine, Mama!* ». She shook her head negatively as if to refute my answer. As the minutes passed, her questions became more in-depth, more intimate. She wanted to know if I had a boyfriend, I said a very ashamed and shy «*yes*». She got up, walked into her kitchen and came back with a big spoon which was used to empty the mortar of its contents. She then asked me: «*Are you pregnant?*» At this question, my blood rushed through my body and I stammered out, «*I... I don't know... I don't know!* ». Still looking soft and calm, my mother's friend wanted to know when my last period was. I said, looking confused: «*It's been a while, Mama* **'Ndongo**. *She went on to say,*» **Dédé**, *you're pregnant.*

This news, which was unknown to me until now, made me very sad; I started to cry because deep down, I had not thought that these exchanges in love would lead me to live such a complex situation. She cleared her throat and asked me not to cry any more, and she continued to talk to me, asking me if my boyfriend's family knew that I was pregnant? My answer was no. I wondered inwardly *«how is it possible that if I myself did not know what I was going through and what the consequences were, how would **Michel's** parents find out?»* My mother's friend invited me to take a test to see if I was really pregnant. When I took the test, I realised that what *Mama'Ndongo* had said was true. I was indeed pregnant and I was five months pregnant.

This was a shock to the whole family, especially to my father who had many plans for me. I was his princess and he wanted me to concentrate on my studies so that I could become an independent woman. He was saddened by the fact that I was in this state at the age of fifteen, an age when I was supposed to be preparing for my future. Despite the disappointment that my pregnancy caused him, my father supported me as if he was the author...

A few months later, **Mary was** born. My daughter arrived at a time when I was out of step with life. She was so small that I was afraid to lose her. She weighed less than two kilos and at the same time I was still in despair because of my mother's death. It was a very difficult experience because I had no one to guide me on how I should behave as a mother. **Mary** was accepted by the whole family. Secretly, I resolved not to have another child soon enough.

Several years after the birth of my daughter, I left for **England**, it was April 1997. Five years after **Mary's** pregnancy, I was feeling the pressure of my grandmother, my mother's mother. She took it upon herself to remind me of the number of years from my daughter's birth to the present. She informed me that it was not advisable for a woman to go

Life and its surprises

so long without getting pregnant again. My grandmother was careful to give me examples, saying: *«You know, child, all the women who waited several years before conceiving had quite difficult deliveries and some of them could not even get pregnant again...»*. I was alarmed by everything she was telling me but my desire to have children with one man was stronger than anything. I was expecting the father of my first child, who was still living in **Cameroon**. After my grandmother's advice, it took me two years to conceive again.

In January 2000, **Michael** came to **England** to join me. I informed him that I wanted to be a mother again. He seemed confused by the need I presented to him. He told me that he was not ready for it and that he wanted me to give him some time to think about it. He had his reasons, which I didn't quite understand, but later I learned from him that after I came to **England** he had been in a relationship which resulted in a son. He said he wanted to concentrate on this child before thinking of having another. I made him understand that this had nothing to do with me because I just wanted to have another baby.

As I took no precautions to avoid pregnancy, I became pregnant. **With the** exception of my partner who was not at all happy, I was high on happiness because, after all the stories my grandmother had told me about the difficulties of procreating after many years of «inactivity», I saw this pregnancy as an achievement. In his anger, **Michel** advised me to have an abortion. He threatened to leave me if I didn't get rid of the pregnancy. Each time he pushed his imagination further. One day he told me that he would tell all our relatives and friends that he was not the author of this pregnancy. In the face of all his threats, I remained unmoved by all the fears that arose inside me. My desire to be a mother again made me stronger. I confided in my grandmother and she was a great support during this period. She said to me one day when I was very upset because of the threats from my child's father: *«You know, my little girl, when a woman decides to have a child, she does it first of all for herself, because some men almost never assume their responsibility... Many women play two roles in the lives of their offspring, that of father and mother. Many women play two roles in the lives of their children, that of father and mother.»* She closed her remarks by saying: *«Your children will be your joy, and tomorrow they will be your strength...».*

My grandmother had prepared me to make a baby for myself and not for a man. I was not affected by the enormous pressure I received from my partner, and I felt free from his threats because in my grandmother I had an unwavering support. Despite the few moments of sadness I felt as a result of my partner's intimidation, I wanted to have this child more than anything. There was no way I was going to have an abortion. I did everything I could to bring **Michel** to the joyful moments that the arrival of a new child brings, but I came up against a wall of anger. He was not ready to take on another pregnancy, and our relationship was plunged into a blatant lack of harmony. To lure him into my world of joy and to allow him to bond with our baby, I invited him to accompany me to prenatal visits, but he always found excuses. Then, on the eve of the ultrasound, I asked him to come with me again and against all expectations, he agreed without any conditions.

In the consulting room, I sat on the medical bed so that the doctor could do the ultrasound. A few minutes later he asked us if we wanted to know the sex of our child, and we both said yes. After a few turns with his machine on my belly, the doctor exclaimed: *«Congratulations, you are going to have a beautiful baby girl!»* My joy was heightened not because we now knew the sex of the baby, but because my baby was healthy. My daughter's daddy, on the other hand, was downcast, as if this announcement had shattered his dreams of having another boy. Seeing that a

Life and its surprises

furious look was forming on my companion's face, the doctor asked him: «*Sir, are you okay?*» Like a good African, **Michel** just «*flicked*». Faced with my companion's attitude, the doctor went on to say: «*Don't you know that the sex of a child is determined by the man's genes? So this girl is from you and not from your partner!*»

He said nothing but jumped up and walked out, more displeased. At this point I could no longer hold back my sadness and began to cry. The doctor consoled me as best he could. This stranger found the right words to silence my pain. When I was calmer, he asked me questions to try to understand what was really going on between my companion and me. I preferred not to talk about it, I just told him that everything would be fine... I took the doctor's last recommendations and then I left the consultation room. **Michel** was waiting for me outside. I touched his shoulder to get him out of the thoughts he was in. He turned to me and asked: «*Can we go home now?*» When I said yes, he got up and walked a few steps in front of me. He did not look at me, as if he wanted to hide his current state.

When we got home, he called his older brother, **Henri** on the phone to get his help. He told him everything that was happening and the decision he had made. I felt that neither of them wanted to understand my reasons for keeping the child. One day, while I was holding on to the happiness that this pregnancy was bringing me, I received a call. When I picked up the phone, I realised that it was **Henri**. I took a deep breath before saying, «*Hello?*»
Henri: *How are you,* **Stephanie**?
Me: *I'm fine, thank you, and you?*
- *I'm still fine, love! But tell me* **Steph** ?
- *Yes ?!*
- *How is it that you oppose your husband's desire to end this pregnancy, don't you think it would be better to preserve the harmony of your rela-*

tionship instead of keeping this child? You know, a child is an agreement between two people, so if your husband is not ready, why not listen to him?

- I hear you **Henri**, but the child is mine and I have decided to keep it for myself and not for your brother. If he doesn't want to take it on as a father, I won't force him. I'm not afraid to look after my daughter on my own. Don't worry about me, **Henri**.

I hung up the phone with these words and continued as if nothing had happened to enjoy my peace. My desire to be a mother again against the advice of my partner and his brother was leading me to an addiction to food.

One day, during an argument, my daughter's father shocked me by saying: *«Listen to me very well, when you have your contractions, you must be outside to call the ambulance because I don't want to see them in this house!»* Thank God he wasn't there when I was in labour pains. So the ambulance drivers were able to come and get me from the house and take me to the hospital.

Jennifer, is the name I gave her, was delivered by caesarean section because her weight, which was almost five kilos, did not allow me to deliver her vaginally. It was quite a difficult experience for me because there was no one to assist me, I was all alone and by the grace of God everything went well. **Jennifer** was very beautiful, she was a photocopy of her daddy. I felt bad that my baby was the spitting image of a man who didn't want her, but that didn't stop me from loving her. A few months after I gave birth, **Henri** came to visit us. I wanted to have a paternity test, but he laughed and said: *«Sister-in-law, it was to get you to have an abortion because he didn't want the baby. I can't make you lose your money. I know, without a doubt, that **Jennifer** is my brother's child. Look *at how she even looks like him. »*

My daughter gave me immense joy, the cheerfulness she exuded made the whole house in which we lived feel full of love. The memory of this period remains painful for me and to avoid sinking back into a couple's war, I put myself on contraceptive pills.

A few months later, I received the sad news that my father had died. It was one pain too many, one wound too many that I had to heal. I couldn't control my emotions because I still wanted my daddy alive. But God had decided otherwise. Sometime before my father's death, **Michel** had left the house because we were experiencing misunderstandings that were not conducive to the smooth functioning of our relationship. In this chaotic sequence, I stopped taking my pill because, even though I was not ready to get pregnant again, I did not have a partner.

Chapter 2
« Never two without three »

«Sometimes we have no choice but to forgive and fall back into the euphemism of a life that could be apparent happiness...»

After a short absence, the father of my children proposed to me to return to our home but I was not able to do him this favour. I loved my partner, but he had a flaw and for me that was his violence. Which was unbearable for me. And in turn, this affected our relationship enormously. My grandmother, to whom I listened a lot, advised me otherwise. She made me understand with solid arguments that I would need **Michel** in many areas of my life. My mother's mother was the only person who could make me change my decisions, which is why I accepted him back into my life. By sharing the same house as this man, I welcomed him into my bed and allowed him to dive back into the depths of my being.

Our life together slowly took off again, and a year after **Jennifer's** birth, I was pregnant again. The trauma of my experience during the pregnancy of our second child made me keep the news secret. I didn't want to go through the turmoil I had experienced earlier, so I made an appointment with the doctor to have an abortion. He set a date that suited my schedule. But only something strange happened because during the night before my abortion appointment, I had a dream in which my late father advised me not to do it and before I woke up he told me in the dream the sex of the baby I was carrying. It was my father coming back to me basically. I loved my dad so much that when I opened my eyes, I was overwhelmed by what I had just seen in my dream. I thought about all my father's words and a feeling of sadness came over me. I had been able to see my father again and he was no longer with us. I had believed in the content of this dream because when he was alive we were very close.

Being a new convert to Christianity, I did not start praying because the spiritual world was still not something that I understood. I contacted the clinic to cancel my appointment, the secretary did not try to understand why, but invited me to contact them in case I changed my mind. I then told my partner that I was pregnant. Unlike **Jennifer**'s pregnancy, **Michel** was enthusiastic about the idea of welcoming a new baby because, I think, he knew that the arrival of this child could rebuild our relationship, which was already in trouble. He supported me like never before so this was the only pregnancy I was happy with. I felt special and every second of it was like a fairy tale. I was fulfilled and it enhanced my outer beauty.

Michel did not want to miss any stage of my pregnancy, and accompanied me to all my meetings with the doctor, as well as to the laboratory for my tests. A few hours before the ultrasound, he asked me to ask the doctor to give us the details of the baby's sex. I didn't agree to this request because I was still traumatised by his behaviour during my last pregnancy, which is why I wanted to keep the suspense to the end. Closer to my due date, my partner paid for me to do my hair so that I can look pretty while I am giving birth.

My companion surprised me even more with his behaviour when I told him that I was in maternity labour. He ran to the shower to freshen up, put on nice clothes and perfume himself... When we arrived at the hospital, I was informed that my delivery would be by caesarean section to minimise the risks of not keeping to the recommended distance between pregnancies. I didn't mind as I had learned from my experience with **Jennifer**. This time I was not alone...

My baby was there, we named him **Stephane**. My son hadn't cried, the midwives had had to prick him to make him react... On his little face, I could see my face associated with his daddy's and I was happy.

Every mum needs to see a bit of herself in her baby's face and my son had that look that I was looking for when I first saw **Jennifer**. The result was a beautiful face that made us want to look at him constantly. Everything went as planned and a few days later we were back home. We were so happy that **Stephane** was such a calm and happy baby that his daddy nicknamed him *«Happy boy».*

Unlike the other babies, **Stéphane did** not cry. I didn't have sleepless nights like when Jennifer was born. With my son, who never cried, I woke up on my own to feed and change him. My routine was this: after bathing him, I would feed him, then turn on the TV and lay him in his cot while I took care of his sister.

Stephane started to sit up when he was three months old, but I noticed that He was not giving eye contact when looking at people, or objects, or at least he had difficulty concentrating. Of the many toys my son had, he was not interested in any of them, which worried me greatly. I began to make comparisons between my daughter and him. When she was the same number of months old, **Jennifer** wanted all the toys that were in front of her and when she couldn't reach one of them, she would use any strategy to get it. I remember her screaming, crying and grabbing my dress when she wanted me to hold her. She would follow me around the house.

I often deliberately did not pay attention to my son for several hours to see how he would react but he remained passive. I also noticed that even when it came to eating, he didn't ask. However, when he was hungry, **Stephane** would put his two fingers in his mouth and start sucking them. At that moment, I went to find him and would try to get a smile out of him but my son remained unperturbed. He didn't look at me, he didn't turn around as I passed. And very often, as I passed him, I would make hand gestures accompanied by a big smile and say: *«Hel-*

lo darling; hello my love; hello...!» But again **Stéphane did** not show any emotion. I sometimes tickled him but my son laughed furtively. He was the complete opposite of **Jennifer** who burst out laughing as she lay down at every face and tickle I made. I was confused by my observation. But his dad was proud that his son was so calm. I wanted my boy to have fun and break everything in his path. Every parent wants to have an active child and be happy with a smile or a cry. Every parent wants to hear their baby cry so they can remember it.

I went to see a paediatrician when **Stephan was** four months old. I told him everything that I found abnormal in my son. The doctor invited me to observe him a little more because he thought it was impossible to diagnose an illness in a child of that age. The paediatrician told me that I was not being kind to complain about a baby's behaviour. He asked me to be more patient because there was nothing wrong with my son. He told me that he would be retiring this month and that I would have a new paediatrician. He told me that I should contact my doctor who could do what was necessary, or refer me if necessary, for any concerns I had with my son. I was reassured that I was wrong to worry about **Stéphane**'s health but my maternal instinct persisted in making me believe that there was indeed a problem with my baby. I went home and tried not to worry about my boy's behaviour.

Six months later, **Stéphane** was crawling. The particularity with him was that he didn't do it to grab an object or a piece of furniture, he just moved forward aimlessly and only when he wanted to. I had to force him to follow me a little to get him to do so, but without paying too much attention. He didn't behave like all the babies who crawled to grab toys or to pull on their parents' clothes. My son had no problems with motor skills or physical development as he was standing and taking his first steps by the time he was eight and a half months old.

I made another appointment when my baby was almost nine months old. When it was my turn to be seen by the doctor, I said: «Good morning sir! «He looked at me as if his mind was elsewhere, and then I added: *«I see that my son still has the same problem».*
Doctor: *Which one?*
Me: *I don't know but I have observed that he doesn't play, doesn't cry...*
- Why do you want your son to cry?
- It's not that I want him to cry, but I want him active
- Madam, try to look at your five fingers. Go ahead, look at them!
I was doing so when he asked me:

- Are your five fingers active?
- Yes
- Do they do the same thing?
- Not really
- You should know that children are not the same. Just be aware that your child has a very special character.

I went home feeling down because I hadn't had any convincing answers, but I knew without a shadow of a doubt that there was something wrong no matter what the doctor said.

By the time **Stephane was** one year and two months old, he was walking very well and his feet were firm on the ground. I went back to the **GP** who was angry with me. He didn't hide his nervousness from me, which is why I told him fearfully: *«My son doesn't talk.»* He opened the baby's mouth and looked at his tongue and said, *«Madam, there is nothing wrong with your son, he will talk when the time is right!»* I let him know that my child did not follow me with his eyes, and then he put his fingers in front of the child's eyes and said: *«Your baby can see perfectly, he has no problem, madam!»* Even today I think that this man thought I was just trying to disturb him because every time I went there he said to me in a bitter tone: *«What is it now? »* ...

Stéphane was two years old and I still could not see any improvement in his behaviour. I went to see this doctor again because I was still waiting for the contact from the new paediatrician without any follow-up. As soon as I said *«Hello Doctor!»* He replied *«Thank you, good morning»* and asked me his favourite question: *«What is it now?»* I replied, *«You told me that the child would change, but to this day I have not seen any improvement in his character. He is not like his sister when she was the same age! He takes a long time to get out of the nappies, it seems he was afraid to use the toilet»* But he retorted: *«Children are not the same. She is a girl and he is a boy»*. This time he referred me to a psychiatric hospital and advised me to do a lot of sport and swimming because he thought I was having a breakdown. When I went there with my son, I was amazed that this appointment was for me. This doctor thought I was crazy! As I tried to figure out what was going on, the nurses told me that this is a psychiatric hospital and that this doctor had referred me there because he thought I had a mental problem. I was shocked by what I was experiencing.

The doctors asked me questions which I was careful to answer. After a long time, I made them understand that my problem was with my baby and that I myself did not have one. The psychiatrists were all amazed by their colleague's attitude and promised to send him a letter in which they would make him understand that I had no psychiatric problem... This experience scared me a lot and I was afraid to go to a hospital again for my son.

I was so confused that I told the people around me to get some direction. But even my grandmother didn't understand what was going on and asked me not to worry because the child was very small to determine if something was wrong. She wanted to see her great-grandson face to face to better understand what I was worried about, but unfortunately at that time I could not move easily. For reasons beyond my control, the renewal of my residence permit was dragging on at immigration.

Everyone was supporting me as best they could but I was still depressed, especially as when I looked around I could not see any child at that age exhibiting the same behaviour I was seeing in **Stephane**. I didn't know what to do because I felt confused and lost...

Chapter 3
« The diagnosis »

«Embarrassing situations arise very often during our earthly journey. The hardest thing is to be confronted with an irrevocable condition. »

One day, I decided to go back to school and, in order to allow **Stéphane to** socialise with children of his own age, I enrolled him in a crèche. The truth is that my son's condition was giving me sleepless nights and I wanted to take advantage of this to change a little. After some time in the nursery, **the manager** invited me to her office to talk, she said. I went there without really knowing why. Once inside, I sat down and we started talking about various topics when she asked me: *«How are you?»* I said, *«Fine, thank you, and you?»* She replied, *«Fine, thank you madam»* and then asked me, *«Has your son been diagnosed yet?* I looked at her with wide eyes and then said, *«Diagnosed with what?»*

The manager*: I don't know but I think your son has a problem.*
Me *(looking at her insistently): Really?*
- Yes, Madam,» she said sadly.
- You see,» I said, «you're the only person who has seen what I've been trying to tell people. But everyone, including my doctor, told me that it was normal and that it was only a matter of time.
- No Madam, it's not a matter of time. Have you contacted a paediatrician?
- Unfortunately for me, the paediatrician in charge of my son has retired. During my last visit, she informed me that another paediatrician would be assigned to me, but until then I am still waiting.

The manager pointed me to a centre where I could self-refer to a specialist. But this place only opens once a week, every Friday from two to five o'clock. It was only Monday evening, and I felt like I was waiting forever. I have a problem with time management, but that day was not the case, because at one o'clock I was already there. I spoke with the medical officers of the centre. I was able to explain everything I had observed in my son. They immediately sent **Stéphane to** a specialised hospital *" Guys and saint Thomas Hospital"* where the first tests were done immediately. It took more than a year of my child's life to find out what was wrong with him. But after each examination, the doctors did not inform me of anything, except that they could not confirm anything at the moment and that it was important for them to do several tests to have a common position on his health. The tests were done three times so that they could be sure of their diagnosis, one of them explained to me.

My baby was over four years old when the doctors made their medical report. I received a phone call during which the secretary informed me of the day of my appointment. She advised me to arrive at the exact time. That day I was going to this place with my partner. After a long speech, one of the doctors, a woman, said to me very tactfully: *«Here you are, madam, we have your son's results in front of us. It appears that you have a child with a complex neurodevelopmental disorder and **ADHD**... In other words, your son is autistic. »*

To tell the truth, it was the first time in my life that I had heard about this disability I asked her in a worried voice what it was in practice. Then, with examples, she made me understand that my baby's behaviour and reactions were those of children with this condition. I was still confused because I still didn't understand what she was explaining. This doctor was unable to enlighten me further. She saw that despite all the words she was using, I did not understand anything.

At the end of our exchange, my interlocutor advised me not to go on **Google** at the risk of coming across false information that would do me more harm than good. Of course, I made her believe that I wouldn't do anything about it. But when I got home, I threw my bag in one of the armchairs and turned on the computer in the living room. I couldn't wait to see what I would find. In the search bar, I typed in the word *«autism»*.

The diagnosis

A whole host of information came up. I read word by word everything that was written about it. I understood that my son had always shown all the symptoms of this condition and that if I had been taken seriously by the previous paediatrician **(GP)**, my baby would have been quickly taken care of... At that time, **Stéphane** was very calm but the only concern I had was his language because it was difficult for him to speak.

When I asked around, I was told that there are autistic people who speak and others who don't, there are those who have problems with mobility, vision, hearing. There are those whose brains are partially or totally affected because most autistic people are epileptic. There are those who were calm, hyper or had a sleeping disorder and so on. But I didn't know which category to put my child in, I didn't know if he would be able to express himself with words or not. From that moment on, I made a point of observing my son more than before. I had reached the point where I knew which of his actions would follow another. So I encouraged my baby to talk, I worked to get my child to develop mentally. It was complicated but for love, a mother will do anything to see her child reach his potential.

After a while, **Stephane**, who was very calm and gentle, became very strong and violent. My son, who used to just suck on his fingers when he was hungry, had reached a stage where he would open and close doors with great force to make noise to show his frustration. He no longer liked certain clothes such as shirts, long-sleeved knitwear, but he had a penchant for short-sleeved T-shirts. He no longer wanted to dress decently. **Stephane** would undress himself after I finished dressing him. I had noticed that my son did not like the label of the clothes he was wearing to touch him and he would put his T-shirt the wrong way round . He liked orange, white and blue clothes. I also noticed that it was a fight to comb his hair. After the bath he would walk on his toes and demand that I give him the clothes he was wearing before his shower because he would never take them off. I had to buy him knitwear of the same texture and colour so that he could easily change.

To prevent him from getting angry, as it was always a difficult time to deal with, I had to do as he wanted at first to prevent any crisis, especially as his difficult times were emotionally difficult for me. Over time, when my child was hungry, he would go into the kitchen and it was up to me to understand that I had to hurry up and give him his meal or offer him something; water or a snack... Very often he would help himself to the fruit basket without asking anyone. This was commendable at first because he didn't have to make noise with the doors, but it made him more reserved.

While waiting for my appointment with the therapist, I started researching online to better understand **autism** and how to support my son. In fact, I had found a lot of information on **google** and **youtube**. But I couldn't apply all the tips and advice that was recommended. I didn't have the courage and I didn't know the techniques to put into practice. I would try something but would quickly give up, I had no patience. My son became violent every time he couldn't express himself. He would scream while closing his ears. He would clap his hands very hard in anger to the point where until now his palms have remained very hard. Sometimes he would throw himself on the floor or even throw everything in his path or in front of him.

Stephane has no sense of danger, he was not afraid of cars. I was afraid to go out with him because I was afraid something bad would happen to him. I was constantly holding his arms for his security, when someone would try and speak to me, I would often focus all of my attention to holding his arms as I feared that he would run away or touch

The diagnosis

something. This alone was draining me both physically and emotionally. At the end of each day I was weary. Stephane was obsessive about peoples' feet, during summer when he sees people wearing open shoes he will go to them and try to play with their feet. I disliked it and I found it embarrassing.

We had one appointment after another with different specialists. We saw a hearing specialist to make sure my son didn't have a hearing problem because he didn't realise when he was being called or when there was noise around him. A physiotherapist to make sure he wasn't hiding a mobility problem. I also made an appointment with an **ENT** specialist to check that his tongue was not the cause of his inability to speak. A psychiatrist for his mental, cognitive or congenital state to finally evaluate his intellectual level.

One day I went with my son to a speech therapist for help. When I explained to her every move my son made when he was hungry or thirsty, she instructed me to hide things he had access to. In this way he would be led to speak up and ask for what he wanted. She made me understand that my son did not ask, because he could see what he needed and that when he no longer had these things in sight, he would begin to express himself verbally or he would find a way to communicate his need. She added that **Stephane**'s brain was not common because the part that motivates him to do it was not active and that was the reason for his silence. She encouraged me to be firm and patient with him. Then I asked her puzzled: *«Will my son ever speak?»* She replied with a not too reassuring look: *«Madam, I don't want to tell you falsehoods to please you. In my career, I have seen all kinds of* **autistic people***, some who spoke at nine, some at thirteen and some a little later. There is no set age at which an* **autistic person will be able to** *express themselves. However, I have seen a few who do not speak verbally at all, but communicate in some way.»*

I was so insistent on my question that she said, *«There are many ways to communicate without speaking, such as sign language or picture exchange: this simple practice involves the child seeing a list of pictures and choosing the one that represents his need. When they give you the picture, you give them the picture representation.»* With her, I learned that most autistic people are visual learners.

So I started taking sign language classes to enable me to communicate with my son. Unfortunately, **Stéphane** could not receive speech and language therapy lessons because the first lessons had to be given before he was five years old, the instructor told me. My son, who was already seven years old, could not hold his gaze, he did not look people in the eye, so sign language was not appropriate for him. I did not lose the motivation to continue the sign language courses. I tried to take these courses at my own expense. I contacted a private language therapist, but it was not easy because there were none available. I was willing to do anything to help my son, I had money to accompany my baby but I couldn't find anyone who could help me, not even in private.
At that time my relationship with the dad took a hit. We decided to separate. I must admit that without emotional support it was not easy. The stress of my son's health was weighing on us.

We had been forced to accept **Stephane's** in his condition. As time went by, he became stronger and his violence increased and frightened many. We knew that those around us were disturbed by this.

I remember this couple meeting we had every month. We would visit each family in the group once a month and take turns. I would go with **Stephane**, but I would always hold him because when he was playing with other children he was rough and the parents didn't like his behaviour very much. I understood them perfectly, which is why I tried to explain to them what was wrong with him. For a parent it is not always acceptable for someone to hurt their offspring for whatever reason. I fully agreed with them but I was overwhelmed by my son's situation myself.

From one day to the next, I found myself excluded from our meetings because, to tell you the truth, the members of my group did not want me in their homes anymore and they no longer came to my home. So I found myself alone. With the exception of a small number of group members, I no longer had any friends. The way people looked at my child made my mother's heart very sad. He was described as ***violent, stubborn, badly brought up, mentally ill***... and all the disproportionate words that could be used to describe his behaviour, but my baby was suffering and I was suffering with him.

But my son was the opposite of what men thought of him. **Stephane** is **autistic**; he and most people with this condition live in a world of their own. Normal people see things as they are, but **autistic** people do not. For example, we can see colours as they are but **autistic** people will think that the colour white is a different shade. It will be quite difficult to change his mind about what he thinks he knows because he is connected to another reality.

When my boy turned nine, I planned a birthday party because I wanted to have all the people I had always shared everything with around me. I wanted those people who had shunned me and always made excuses on my phone calls to them to come and take part in this event with us. I had invited some nice people and in order not to be short of something, I bought some excess drinks and made enough food. But my disappointment was great because none of my friends came to the party. I found myself with people who didn't really know me. Indeed, it was my colleagues who had accepted my invitation. As for my long-time friends, some of them came alone without children and without their spouses, who had stayed at home to look after their children. This party, which had been organised for a child, was only composed of adults, there were no children. My son was alone with no one to play with. I hired a big bouncy castle, someone to paint the children's faces, prepared lots of activities for children and a lot of party bags. His birthday was turned into a party for grown-ups. I was deeply saddened by this.

This step made me realise that I had to come to terms with the fact that I no longer had any friends. I had to face the fact that I had to live my life without them. It was painful but for my own happiness I had to get used to it. I accepted life as it was, without my friends, without a companion. There was no one who could understand what I was going through.

Chapter 4
« The impact in my family »

«Every wound leaves a scar and every scar tells a story. A story that says: I survived.

Stéphane's condition has had a negative impact on our family life and on my relationship. It's true that my partner and I didn't go out enough, but he didn't even give us time to sit down and take care of ourselves or our two daughters. This created a stressful situation that affected even our intimate life. I remember times when even at the end of the day I would be in bed crying. His father would go to bed before me most of the time. For me, it was necessary for **Stéphan**e to be asleep for me to try to get back to my room. Once I was lying down, **Michel** wanted to destress by being intimate. We had a big problem because I was so emotionally and morally exhausted that I could not satisfy him. And this created a tension that did not help us as a couple. My relationship with him took a hit. Little by little the intimate desire disappeared in me. This situation created so much tension that my partner accused me of being unfaithful in order to break me down. Our relationship was further paralysed.

As my partner and I were only focused on our son, the parent-child relationship we had with our daughters, **Marie** and **Jennifer**, became more fragile. **Michel** and I were more focused on our son because autistic children are different children, and they need much more physical, moral, emotional attention etc. and the condition of **Stéphane**, our son, saddened us the most. But we didn't understand the need to keep the link we had with our daughters, because of their «normal» state, we thought they understood that, and we thought that they needed our attention less, but we were quite wrong. We were making a crucial mistake. Every child needs to feel the presence of their parents in their lives, but when their parents give all their time and energy to another child, this creates a situation of jealousy, revolt and sometimes anger. This exasperation may well give way to hatred.

In 2006, when **Stéphane's** health diagnosis had just been discovered, I was trying to understand what our new life should be: how I should manage the condition of my son, my two daughters and my couple. I myself was lost in a world I didn't understand enough. **It should be** noted that before my son's diagnosis, I had never heard of **autism** and I didn't even know what it was. **YouTube** back then was not like it is today with all the information.

While I was going through these dark moments in my life, I became ill. At my appointment with the doctor, he told me that I had **malaria**. As a result, I was interned for ten days, almost two weeks. These were difficult times for me because, in order to reduce contamination, I was not allowed to be visited. **Marie**, for example, could not come to see me. Only their father was allowed to do so.

The day after I was discharged from hospital, my eldest daughter came to tell me that she wanted to speak to me. I still remember the day she came to my room with an anxious and uncertain look on her face and said, «*Mum, I want to talk to you.*» I looked up and listened to her. The look in her eyes told me that there was a problem. So I asked her if she was okay. With her shoulders, she gestured as if to say she didn't know. I invited her to come into my arms and then I said, «*It's okay, honey! Tell me what's wrong.*» She replied, «*I'm pregnant.*» This news made me even more fragile. As I tried to integrate the news into my brain, I asked her, «*Who told you you're pregnant?*» She replied, «*Mom, I was at the hospital for a pregnancy test... I'm pregnant.*» She looked at me furtively because she was afraid of my reaction. I had the strength to ask her how she ended up in the hospital for a pregnancy test?

She informed me that the mother of the boy responsible for the pregnancy is a nurse. While I was in hospital, she went to see her to do some tests that determined her condition. In shock, I looked up at my

The impact in my family

daughter hoping she would tell me it was a joke. But nothing happened. While I was still in a joke, She told me about the decision she had made to keep the baby. I was stunned by what I heard from my 14-year-old daughter, I felt betrayed. I understood immediately that she was just telling me what her decision was. As a young mother myself , I was more worried about her future. I wondered if **Mary** understood that I was exhausted by her brother's condition.

I remember well that sometimes there were occasions when we sent her on a few errands, she would take a long time. I put it down to puberty and no more. Before **Stéphane** was born, **Marie** and I were very close, so I thought that my daughter would not hide such a relationship from me.

She was so proud of her pregnancy because it would allow her to be closer to the man she loved the most, her son's father, since at home everything revolved around **Stéphane**. At the same time, I projected myself back several years when my father learned from *mama* **Ndongo** that I was expecting a child. I understood how he felt because I was going through the same thing myself.

With every word that came out of her mouth, whose condescension echoed in my ears, I was carried away by a dizziness that almost made me faint. I think she understood that I was not well because she was now looking at me with concern, but my daughter did not dare to ask me what was going on. At that very moment I was feeling disillusioned with life. I hadn't noticed that my baby, only fourteen years old, had taken the most delicate step in a young girl's life. *«But how did this happen? How could I have failed to see something so obvious? Why, seeing her age, had I not taken the time to explain to her how she could avoid early pregnancies? »*

The truth is that **Marie** was discreet, like all girls of her age. Not only was she very small in body, she only had two good friends that I knew and they were all girls from decent background and I knew their parents. As a child, my older daughter was very quiet and peaceful, obedient and also smart at school. I don't even know where the time came for her to meet her boyfriend.

I remember almost two years ago before she got pregnant, she asked me this: *«Mom, how do I know when a woman is fertile? I want to know so I know when to have sex without getting pregnant?»* I, naively, thought that my daughter just wanted to know. Nevertheless, I asked her if she had a boyfriend. She answered in the negative and then added that she was asking me out of pure curiosity. So with great calm and kindness, I told her not to bother. I would give her all the information about this area at the appropriate time.

I was asking myself a lot of questions that left me with more questions. I felt as if the sky was falling on me, I was caught between two fires because on the one hand there was **Stéphane** who suffered from **autism** and on the other hand there was his sister who was pregnant. **Marie** later told me that she had become close to this young boy and then given herself over to him because he gave her his time. She let me know that she needed to talk to someone outside our family to explain everything she was going through in the house and how my relationship with her father and her brother's condition were affecting her. Which was the opposite with us because we made her feel less interested in what she was going through. She felt neglected by us, her parents, and she needed us to listen to her from time to time. She just wanted our attention and I understood that the condition my son was in meant that everyone was seeking comfort in their own way.

The impact in my family

In her language and decisions, it was clear to understand that my older daughter was looking for a way out. Perhaps **Stéphane's** condition was affecting her too. But she was more concerned with her own problems of how to get out of her circumstances where all her parents' attention was directed to one child because of his condition.

Jennifer, who was only one year and nine months older than **Stephane**, let me know by her behaviour that she wanted me to be more present at her side. She wanted me to hold her long enough as I did with her brother. My second daughter didn't have enough of our time because my son was asking too much of us. She too was beginning to demand attention. She cried when she needed something, I think she realised that this was how she could get my attention.

As she grew older, **Jennifer** told me that her brother's condition had a big impact on their relationship. On several occasions, she told me how she felt that **autism** had taken her place in her brother's life. Sshe wanted to have a close relationship with him, especially he is her only brother. She wanted to talk about puberty with him. She wanted to be very close to him to find out if he had any girlfriends etc.

Their father, on the other hand, did not hesitate to have a glass of wine whenever the opportunity arose.

I was terribly angry at myself for leaving my daughters behind, the consequence before my eyes was alarming. But it was almost impossible to realise the opposite as I was always in hospital with my son and when we were at home I always had to check that he wasn't harming himself. Unfortunately, sometimes he would hurt himself. And as he hardly ever cried I could only see it later.

Our friends had all abandoned us, we were left with almost no one who could give us honest criticism of the way we were handling our children. There was no one to support us, no one to let us know how we should behave, no one to make us aware of the mistake we were making by focusing only on **Stéphane**. We were in a spiral that was tightening on me.

Because of the stress linked to the fact that we thought that our son might not speak, and that I too refused to accept his condition, a distance was gradually growing between **Michel** and me. We were losing the closeness that had kept us together until now. The father of my children and I were no longer on the same wavelength. A question or a remark was now the subject of a strong argument that led us into a spiral of misunderstandings. My husband and I were at the end of our rope and the best option for us was to put our relationship on hold. During another argument in 2008 my husband left the family home. This was just few months after the birth of our grandson. I was alone, once again, with a child with special needs, my first daughter who had just had our first grandchild, and **Jennifer** who also needed me. It must be said that **Marie's** early pregnancy did not help to better my current situation and especially in our relationship. The father of my children had a hard time with the fact that his little girl was pregnant at a very young age and he was throwing stones at me and accusing me of not being firm enough with her from the start. He blamed me for this situation for very long time.

I thought that this separation would help us to understand that we were better together, which is why I was not worried about him leaving. At first I thought **Michael** loved me and his children so much. Especially his Happy boy, our son. I remained confident that this break-up would not go any further than that. Just a break-up. I thought he would call me one morning to tell me that he was tired of being away from his family, and would come home. But I was wrong.

One day, as I was thinking about my youth, I was brought out of my thoughts by the sound of the bell. I ran to open the door but found myself face to face with a stranger who was handing me a document on which I had to sign. I did so with great hesitation and when I handed it to him, he gave me a large envelope and, after wishing me a good day, he took his leave.

When I had closed the door, I opened the envelope. I was astonished to find that the letter was actually a divorce letter. I let out a cry of pain that frightened my children. I couldn't believe that **Michael** could do such a thing to me, as if he was only thinking about himself and had forgotten that we were a family. I was so devastated that I burst into tears. I hoped that he would have understood why my behaviour towards him had changed. I thought my husband would have fought for us, and decided to be a better person for our children.

Before signing, I contacted a lawyer because I wanted to get an expert opinion. The lawyer used simple words to make me understand what was best for me to do. The lawyer advised me to start a mediation process for a possible reconciliation, if I did not want to divorce.

Michel had moved to **Birmingham**, a city in the north of the West **Midlands** region of **England**, where he lived with his friends. Many of them and even some of his friends encouraged him in the decision he had made.

So I resolved to go and join him. But before doing so, I gave him a call. No sooner had I made the call than he picked up the phone. I was

greeted by a calm, gentle voice, which I was probably getting out of boredom. He said, *«Hello, **Stephanie**?»* I answered in a small voice and said, *«Yes darling, how are you? »*
- I'm fine. Are you and the kids okay?
- Yes, we are fine. Darling, I'm calling because I've received the divorce letter and I'd like to discuss it in person, please?

He merely agreed without objection and then I suggested that I go to **Birmingham to** see him.

In order not to leave my children alone, I paid for the services of a nanny who would take care of my babies. I booked a room at the local **«Ibis»** hotel. For my stay with the father of my children, I paid for a couple's service, a special decoration. In our room, I explained to them that it was a unique moment that we were celebrating without giving them any details, as if we were having our wedding night.

I booked my train ticket, and got ready for my trip to Birmingham to travel. I looked in my wardrobe and chose the best outfits that I knew would remind my husband of the great moments we had together and change his mind. The journey is usually around 2 hours, but for me on this occasion it seemed to be very long. I had a mix of emotions because I was wondering what if all this is a waste….., Nevertheless I remained positive and I was telling myself that I was doing this to save my family. I was looking good and very elegant; the smell of my perfume was great. On the train people were looking at me with a great envy, but I was a broken inside.

I arrived in this city of **Birmingham** with the hope of rebuilding my marriage and I was determined to do so. I contacted the father of my children to inform him of my arrival. I dictated my details to him and a few moments later we were together. Presumably he had prepared to receive me. He took me to a restaurant where we ate, drank and above all laughed as if our relationship was not on the verge of breaking up. I saw in this man the person he had always been, someone kind and funny, and this aspect made me more optimistic.

That night we had a nice, sweet night. I was happy to be in his arms again.

The desire that had left me returned without any effort. We were so appeased to be together again that we could not take our eyes off each other. The next day we woke up at about twelve o'clock, so long had the night been. We had been silent for several minutes when I said to him, «Darling, I have received the divorce letter. But I'm having trouble sending it back to you. *«He looked at me with wide eyes and then said, «Why don't you want to? »*

I was very surprised by his question but I decided to keep calm and answer him gently, I said: *«Because I still love you and we all miss you. Honey, please come home. The children and I need you. »*
He was silent as if he was thinking about how to answer me and I kept talking saying, *«Think about yesterday dear, remember all we have been through together. You have always been there for me how would I live and move on without you? »*
He cleared his throat and said, *«Stephanie, you're only going to get a divorce. Even if we are to get back together, we have to get a divorce first.»*
As I listened to this answer, I felt my being weaken. I could not hold back my tears because, at that very moment, I thought that all my hopes were in vain. Then he spoke again and said, as if to soothe me: *«Why are you sad? Haven't you ever seen couples break up and remarry a few years later?»* I said in amazement: *«Oh, is that what you want for us?»* He told me, with a touch of anger, to accept only the divorce and then we'll see.

I returned to **London** dejected with the weight of my failed attempt on my shoulders. It was too painful a return for me. I was in tears the whole way. Nevertheless, I made another trip this time to try to make him see reason, but **Michel** was adamant that I sign the document. This time, I resolved to comply because I was not going to force him to stay with me. The truth is, I didn't blame myself for anything, but I was ashamed of the divorce. It was a taboo subject in my family and even in my community... Despite the difficulties I was going through, I wanted to give my children the chance to have their father in their lives and to benefit from his presence. I could see that he enjoyed my company, but he just didn't want to come home anymore. I wasn't ready to be his girlfriend again. The father of my children avoided everything that happened at home; from our son's condition to our daughter's new status. In those days, it was the failure of parents when their daughter gave birth at that age.

When our divorce was finalized, I focused more on my children, leaving aside all the pain that could result from my new life as a *«single woman»*.

I was surrounded by my three children and my grandson Jaydon. I felt loved by all of them and this affection was like a compensation for a love that I thought would last forever.

There were nights when we all slept in my big bed, watching films. The early days were not easy. I had moments of great depression. But by the grace of God, I came to understand that my children needed me. Every time I looked around, I saw that I was the only captain of my ship. If anything happened to me, my children would be the first to lose. So I took my courage in both hands and little by little, I took the road again. As I turned the page, I learned that my happiness depended only on myself and nobody else. I changed the page on which my love story was written and focused on myself, my children and my grandson.

Chapter 5
« Acceptance and Compliance »

«Life as a «divorced mother» is not a restful one. You approach it differently, you take the time to listen to yourself and then you realise that it is better to pick yourself up and appreciate yourself more so that you don't appear weak to your children. We need to be the best role model for them to look up to. »

Despite the loneliness that weighed on me daily, I continued to fight for my children. I was more considerate where once I passed the torch to my partner. I relearned to take time with those who were now my strength. It is true that they have always been, but this time things seemed clearer, as if their father's departure had helped me understand that life was worth living with those around us, no matter what the circumstances. I am not saying that his departure was wanted, but it brought me the closest to my children. I remember the times when we spent nights in my bed. The little ones all liked to be in my room, so much so that I sometimes used it to get them to do better at school etc. I also took this time to rediscover myself and to bring out the talents that were buried inside me.

There were many beautiful people around me. I was overwhelmed by their presence, which amazed me more and more every day. I got to know them better and understand each one with their differences. My grandson **Jaydon**, who was there with us, brought a new energy to the house, a new dynamism. His language, which very often let out a few shrill cries, made us all burst out laughing. And during those moments when only joy was noticeable, I took the trouble to look each of them in the eye to harvest what is the essence of true love.

Jennifer was her usual self. A proud little girl who handled her toys with great care with her small hands. As I watched her with her dolls, I could see that time is not a burden when you love what you do. It was difficult to make her understand that **Jaydon** was not one of her toys because she was always trying to get him to take the dinette. It was so much fun to watch her grumble when **Marie** said *«No* **Jen***, he's my baby and not your toy!»*

As for **Stéphane**, he was giving me a different image than the one I had always wanted to see. I realised in my heart that I had fought until now to make my son the person he was not. I was trying in every way to get him to become a *«normal child»* but I was making a big mistake. It was up to me to adapt to his condition and accept my son that way. It was up to me to understand that my son was special and therefore needed special treatment. So, I took my time and every minute counted. I set myself the goal of understanding him better so that I could accept his condition, which I thought was reversible.

I realised that in order to better help my son, I needed more time. So I reduced my working hours to eighteen hours because they were thirty-two hours a week. And I must admit that for more than twelve years I have never worked full time because my whole life revolves around my son. There are even opportunities for promotion at my job. Since I am not free because of my son, I prefer not to be interested because I have to go to his school to look for him. When he is not in school, I have to stay at home with him. It is difficult for me to find a full-time nanny for him. This new way of looking at my son led me to adapt better to his disability. It also allowed me to help him develop as he is.

I was trying by all means to educate myself about autism, I wanted to understand better to have a better approach to this condition. I tried to live in his world; feeling things the way he felt them, seeing and understanding certain situations the way he did, could only bring me closer to **Stéphane**.

What was most important to me was to learn how to calm him down during his tantrums. By observing my son, I learned that in order to keep him in a peaceful attitude, I had to take him to the park and make him spend at least three hours playing. And after he had played energetically in the park, he could finally sleep at night because his were very restless. He did not usually sleep every night and when he did, he could sleep for two hours. When he was awake, **Stephane** spent it laughing and trying to play. Yet this was the time when we were supposed to be resting, but again it was a challenge for my boy. By learning more about **autism**, I was able to enter into my boy's world and from there I was able to assist him better.

My greatest fear is when we are in public and Stephane finds himself in an unsafe situation. Because he has no sense of danger, when he is in front of a dog no matter the size of the dog. Small, big, muzzled or not, my child would run towards it without fear. He's not even afraid that the dog would bite him. As long as he could have fun he didn't care. He was also fascinated by the sight of my neighbour's dogs. These animals were so big that they scared everyone, but not my son. I was so afraid for his life that I had to extend the fence a little higher so that he would not be able to reach them.

The scariest thing was when we were at home, we had to adjust the windows because we were in constant fear that he would open them and climb over. He would stand on the banisters and start jumping. We had shaped the house to allow my son to be safe. He doesn't cry when he scratches his skin, you can only see that he is bleeding and you couldn't tell when it had happened.

I remember one day I went to pick him up at the end of the day at his school. That day I had arrived a bit earlier than usual. They had all gone out for a walk to discover the bookshop or the parks... I was very disappointed to find that my son had a rope around his back like an animal. When I asked what the rope was for. His teacher told me that she was doing it for his safety because, according to her, they were afraid that my son would hurt himself or bully another child. I was so saddened that I decided to do everything I could to support him. From that day on, whenever my boy had a problem, I did everything to support him and find a solution, instead of feeling sorry for him.

Every time we went out, I grabbed **Stephane** by the arm without distraction because he didn't understand the procedure for crossing the road safely.

This period of loneliness made me know a little more about **autism**. From then on, I knew how to calm him down. I had to get on the same level as him to talk to him; crouch or kneel down, which would help me get his attention and make eye contact. Even though he always looked away from me, I always managed to look him in the eye. To help him improve his communication, I now had to use simple language and short sentences.

I used to name the fruits he pointed to so that he could remember them and in turn, he could name them as well. At the beginning of this exercise, my son did not say anything despite all my efforts, but one day when I kept repeating the word *«banana»*, **Stephane** said *«nana»*. It was like the beginning of a victory for me. Even though I let him know that it was the wrong pronunciation, I was delighted by the step he had just taken. The teachers and health professionals encouraged me not to give up because sooner or later I would be satisfied with my efforts. I thought he couldn't understand what I was saying to him. I started to get much more involved in verbal exchanges even though I didn't get a response from my son, I understood that he could hear what I was saying to him.

As he liked to use the computer, tablet and listen to music from the TV while eating fruit, I managed to put this fruit basket up high so that I could get him to ask. This helped to stimulate his communication. I had the television set placed higher on the wall so that he would not turn it on without my consent, I hid the remote controls. This way of doing things, which had been advised to me by his paediatrician, had a positive impact because when he needed something he came to where I was and took me where he wanted. And, using my hand, my son would point to what he needed at the time.

So I took the opportunity to talk to him and say: «***Stephane**, do you need mum?*» At the time, he didn't even pay attention to what I was saying. But I knew that sooner or later he would end up repeating what he heard.

For several years, I encouraged him to repeat the words after me without ever losing patience. Whenever I had to give him what he wanted, I would say the same word several times and encourage him to repeat it before I gave it to him. With time I insisted that if he doesn't say mum, I will not respond his request. After so many attempts. One day my son said mum. He can now also clearly say mummy and please. We are focusing on one word at a time because I don't want him to be confused.

As I already knew most of the things **Stephane** was interested in, I introduced the method of exchanging pictures. I put the cards with the picture of the object of whatever he kept asking for on one side and the name or word on the other. All he had to do was give me the card representing what he wanted, then I would turn it around and read it to him, then I would encourage him to read with me, and I had to be patient and give him time to repeat the words in his own way.

Following this wonderful development, I started to read him children's stories. He would respond with laughter or a surprised look.

Autism Why My Son

Over time, my son would give me books to read to him. I think he loved reading because he could immerse himself in the world of the story being told. His love of reading made him more passive. Over time he began to repeat the words. When he did something stupid and I said to him: «***Stephane**, no!*» He would repeat «no» with a sad facial expression.

After a while I noticed that my son was a fan of feet. He liked to touch them and it was unpleasant for everyone. But no one could change that because most people with **autism** have a penchant. Unfortunately, my son's weakness made everyone uncomfortable. I used to enjoy watching his various quirks. The way he walked was so amazing that I laughed at first. When he moved, Stephane did so on the tips of his toes like a ballerina, despite the fact that we put extras in his shoes. But as time went on it became worrying. I did everything I could to get my son to behave properly to the point of going to a different doctor. But my efforts were in vain. As a result, his feet became deformed so that even today my son is only wearing tennis shoes because he feels uncomfortable in other types of shoes.

When I went out with him and he heard noise, he would cover his ears with both hands. When he was in a place where there were several people, he did not want to be there. He would immediately try to leave that place, always closing his ears. I remember that at that time, I almost stopped going to church because, when I entered the church with my son, he would scream so loudly that everyone in the room would turn around and look at me with unpleasant eyes and this saddened me so much that, to avoid being distressed, I limited my attendance to the services. It didn't help that sometimes I needed to be with my brothers in Christ for a time of sharing, but alas!

The older my boy got, the more I discovered another side of his personality. By the age of nine, he had stopped showing any form of aggression. Because his communication started to improve without him being able to express himself verbally, my son had developed a form of understanding. **Stephane** became the sweet little child I had given birth to. During this period, he made efforts to express himself. Despite the fact that he did not articulate words well, my child tried to say what he needed. Although it was sometimes very difficult for the people who met him to understand him, in the end he managed to convey his concerns or desires orally, the result made him very proud of his efforts. My child has come a long way.

Some **Autistic** people like to have repetitive and planed schedule . They do not feel very relaxed about changing their habits. You need to prepare them in advance for any change.

My son never ceased to impress me; he had developed a passion for cycling, which he does very well. He also enjoyed swimming. This led me to take him to the pool quite frequently so that he could practice one of his favourite sports. He was, and continues to be, passionate about electronic devices *« iPads, computers, and phones that he particularly uses either for listening to music or for games»*. Everything followed in quick succession and gradually **Stephane** became emotional. He laughed when he saw funny scenes but only cried when he had a sore body part.

It was small but so big for me and this development made us very happy.

Chapter 6
« New momentum »

«*Despite the length of the night, the day finally dawned. Little by little I no longer considered Stéphane's condition a curse or a problem. This allowed me to give a new impetus to my life. I adjusted everything around me so that my children were my priority. I had to consider my son as a normal person and offer each one his time and place. This gave me time to take care of myself again, because after all, life is ahead. This is how I met a man who accepted me and my children. A few years later, I became pregnant.* »

This period, which I particularly liked, became very stressful because I was afraid of giving birth to another child who would have the same disability as **Stephane**. The doctors did not help matters when they informed me that there was a high risk if my boy's **autism** genes came from me. In that case, the likelihood of me having another **autistic child** was high. But I was convinced that everything would be fine. However, the specialists reassured me that having a new baby could help him enormously. So I was mentally fighting the thoughts that made me think it was a mistake to keep this child or that my baby could be **autistic**. The truth is that I know parents who have two or even three children, all of whom are autistic, and this is really hard.

When I reached my seventh month and my child was stirring in my womb, I took **Stephane** by the arm and, put his hand on my belly, I let him know that inside me a person was growing who would enlarge our family. I told him that this baby would not take his place but would add to our lives. He looked at me with a lost look. This saddened my heart but I remained strong because I knew in my heart that he would understand in time. I continued to tell him that his sister was in my belly and showed him videos of babies. Luckily for me he finally understood. But my only problem now is that whenever stephane sees me or any person with a big belly no matter if they are male or female, he will point to them by saying mommy Baby, baby. I have to tell him that it is not baby and sometimes he appeared to be confused, I could tell by the look on his face that he didn't understand much of the message.

Eliza was born on a sunny morning. My delivery went perfectly. I remember that before she came out of my womb, I was panicked that I wouldn't hear her crying because for me, her cry was a kind of guarantee that my daughter was healthy. She looked so beautiful in her new-born clothes that I couldn't take my eyes off her. When the midwife handed her over to me, I was overcome with emotion. Indeed, as I held my daughter, a great sadness took hold of my heart and I began to cry my eyes out, probably because I had stored up too much fear inside me.

My newborn was finally here and her mission was to bond with her brother. When **Eliza was** a few days old and I was back home, I put her in her brother's arms to see how he would react. When she was in his arms, Stephane did not hold her carefully. Fortunately for us, I was never far away when he had his sister with him. I remember the first time I made him carry his sister. **Stephane** held her *with a fearful air. It was as if he thought he had a doll* in his arms. With great delicacy, I took her from his hands without much delay. And I didn't make a fuss about it.

But with time, **Stephane** came to understand that she is indeed his little sister. He began to treat her with some affection. I did everything to create a relationship between the two. Sometimes I invited him to assist me when I fed his sister and I made sure he was present when I bathed **Eliza**. This was so that he would understand that his sister is like him too.

As **Eliza** grew up, she had many questions because she noticed that he never answered her questions promptly. One day, while they were sitting and she was staring at him, she jumped up and ran to me. When she was close, she stood behind me, wrapped her little arms around me and said, trying to whisper: «*Mum, why doesn't **Stephane** speak, why doesn't he go to school alone and then tell me, Mum, why doesn't he play* with me even though I'm his sister? And then, why do you always have to accompany him to school even though he is old enough to go alone?»*

From the bottom of my heart I was very saddened by her questions. But I took the courage to explain this to her, especially since this was the first time she had this concern. But she didn't understand what I was trying to say about her brother being **autistic**. So I took the opportunity to make this point clear to her again.

When she stopped talking, I put her on my lap and explained in detail why her brother was behaving differently from all the other children. **Eliza**, who did not fully understand what I was saying, was very sad to hear what was coming out of my mouth. My little girl had both hands on her chest and a far-away look on her face as if she was thinking about how she should act to help her brother.

Then she asked me: *«But tell me, Mum, when will Stephane speak properly like us?»*

I told her the truth about my ignorance on this issue, but I also told her that she should know that her brother loves her despite his disability. I tell her that in life, some people talk and others don't. But everyone needs to be loved and treated the same. I made her understand that all we have to do is to love **Stephane** as he is, and to give him all our love because only time will tell when he will speak and what means of communication he will use. The most important thing was that her brother adopted a way of communicating. When I asked her if she also felt love for him, she said an enthusiastic *«yes»*. Then she got up to give him a big hug and came back to sit next to me and **Stephane** was in front of her.

After that, I took the time to observe **Eliza** and her brother. I had the impression that she didn't really know how to approach him, but then the magic started to work. These two people, who were the opposite of each other, formed over time a complementarity that I had never seen before with any of my children. The harmony that emerges from their agreement is so perfect that I almost regret not having had another child earlier because it would have helped **Stephane** to evolve despite his handicap.

Over time, **Eliza** would involve her brother in her most childish games and invite him to repeat after her every word she said. He looked lost at first, but then he began to make an effort to pronounce them. I could see my son with his mouth all agape as he tried to say what his sister wanted to hear. With big gestures, she would let him know that he could manage to push himself to get those words out that seemed difficult. Seeing them play with their words gave me hope for what it might lead to in time. If I hadn't made that last baby, there would be no one who could get on the same level as **Stephane** to help him develop his language and his mind.

Eliza is a very affectionate person, so she takes every moment with her brother to heart. By inviting him to play with her, she was able to help him develop certain emotional, mental and physical skills. For example, she got her brother to say «no» instead of crying when he didn't want to play. She also got him to engage in certain games such as hide-and-seek, and to share and socialise not only with her, but also with people around him.

With my son I tried everything to get him to talk but I couldn't, probably because in his eyes, **Stephane** saw me as his mother, as a superior from whom he had to take orders, and that seemed to be a brake on his evolution. But his little sister came to destroy part of the world in which my boy found himself in order to give him access to reality. It was nice to see someone understand my son, it was reassuring to see someone other than me pay so much attention to him. Their understanding embellished my heart. I enjoyed watching them, I must admit I am really proud of **Eliza**.

I must also say that **Jennifer** was equally a great support in her brother's condition, she was always there for him, even when no one was around. The arrival of **Eliza** meant that **Jennifer** handed over the reins to her little sister. Through **Stephane**'s condition, my youngest daughter has developed a form of leadership character. She is stronger emotionally and mentally than some children of her age, she has developed the courage of a lioness. She speaks with authority, which I never observed with her sisters when they were her age. She is shy, but overly affectionate and strong and speaks freely in public about any subject. She is not ashamed of her brother's condition as she even talks about it to her friends at school and explains to others how she plays with him despite his condition. Indeed, **Stephane**'s condition does not prevent **Eliza from** commissioning her brother for the moment. When he is older, she will probably need his advice.

With his little sister, everything was different. **Stephane** often played a game that represented the family and his attitude showed that he liked to re-enact all the moments we shared when we were all together. His ability to memorise every gesture his dad made towards them was amazing. It was as if my son was studying every move his father made and then repeating them in that game he loved so much.

During these games, **Eliza** was in charge. She knew exactly how to talk her brother into doing exactly what she wanted him to do.

Watching them play together was like watching a movie made by children for children. The scenario I was watching made me laugh out loud very often. My daughter took time to prepare for the occasion. She would come to me with scarves for me to tie around her waist and on her head so that she would fit in perfectly as the African mother. As soon as she had her outfit on, she invited her brother to take his place. She would pick up one of her dolls and imitate a baby's cry, then stop and say to her playmate: «***Stephane***, *prepare the baby's bottle;* ***Stephane*** *gives the baby milk;* ***Stephane*** *changes his nappy...* »

I could see my son running around trying to please his sister who was pretending to stir an imaginary meal. She would occasionally turn to me to see if I was watching them. Sometimes she would go into the kitchen to get either a banana or an apple, which she would cut up and put in her plate to make the game more real.

Eliza had the ability to open my eyes by offering me ideas on what I needed to do in order to take her brother to the next level in his behaviour. I remember the day she came to me and said: «*Mum, tell me, as* ***Stephane*** *plays with me he is not autistic anymore, is he?* »

To my half-affirmative, half-negative answer, she added: «*But why do you still feel obliged to accompany him to school?* »

I replied by saying: «*Given his disability, I don't feel confident to let him go alone because I am afraid of what might happen to him once he is on the street alone.* »

My son, who did not feel comfortable with strangers, could become agitated if there was a problem and plunge into a reactionary crisis during his journey. I have to say that this is my biggest fear till this day. I couldn't imagine how I would feel if something happened to him if I decided to let him go to his school alone. I didn't even want to think about it. But my ally in my fight for my son's behavioural development wanted to see his brother independent and I had no choice but to give in to his advice.

Had it not been for the containment that was put in place to stop the evolution of the **covid-19** pandemic, I would have introduced **Stephane** to being independent. But once the sanitary measures were eased, I started sending **Eliza**, that little girl who is so resourceful with her brother, to run some errands for me in the grocery shop near the house so that he would start to feel comfortable outside and without me.

I remember the day when the milk was all finished at home when **Eliza** and her brother wanted to have their Saturday breakfast. I informed them that they would have to make do with the bottom of the bottle, as I could not go shopping until the afternoon. So she offered to go and buy some from the shop not far from the house. But I said to her: *«No, darling, you are still too young to go into the shop alone.»* Without hesitating, she answered me by saying: *«But Mum, I can go with Stephane. He's grown up, don't worry, I'll speak for him. Believe me Mum, everything will be fine, trust us!»* At the time I was confused. I didn't know if I should let them go or not, so I decided to kill the fear in me. I decided to follow them discreetly, to the shop, to see how they would manage. My daughter was holding her brother by the hand. I saw that she had taken the trouble to hang the shopping bag on his shoulder... When I saw my children coming from a distance, I hurried to the house so that they would not suspect anything. I could hear the sound of their hurried steps as if they had been running. Once they had passed through the front door, **Eliza** and **Stephane** burst into an interminable fit of laughter...

When they were near me, **Eliza** said, while kissing **Stephane**: *«Mum, we did it. You see, you have to trust us!»* Her big brother didn't really understand why his sister was so happy. So, I went up to him, kissed him back, and said: *«Well done son, you went to buy milk with your sister!»* My boy immediately began to repeat my words. I felt a joy in myself and a sense of achievement. It is true that there is still a lot to do in **Stephane**'s life. But I have learned to love him as he is. Today he uses *picture exchange* to communicate. He is more verbal every day and when someone doesn't understand what he wants to say, he immediately starts writing it down, even though his writing is not that clear he will try his best. A few years ago, I couldn't imagine that my boy could do this.

Some people ask me if **autism is** curable? To my knowledge I don't think so. But I am convinced that the conditions of autism can improve with time if we give them the right support. We must remember that there are **autistic people who have not been** diagnosed.

Today, **Stephane** is a big boy and is already becoming a man. This does not prevent me from continuing to take care of his hygiene. He is very happy when I accompany him to the hairdresser, though this was not the case a few years ago. At weekends, I supervise him while he showers. Stephane has become very particular about his hygiene, to the point that he cannot spend a day without taking a bath or a shower. During his puberty stages, I had to teach him how to maintain his hygiene with hair removal. He once tried to cut his own hair and let's just say that it was a fun experience!

Stephane still struggling with a lot including educationally, privacy ect… I learn to appreciate life and my son the way he is and to understand that no one in this life is perfect.

I did what I could do as a mother. Now I let the creator do the rest. I love my son and I would never change him for another child.

Conclusion

«It would be a mistake to believe that we can be free from tragedy. Covid19 taught us a big lesson. We must understand that every Man becomes stronger when he decides to go back to his creator because he alone has the ability to steer the boat in the most surprising way...» Weeping may tarry for the night, but joy comes with the morning.

When we are faced with an anomaly, it feels like the sky is falling, because the dream of almost every parent is to see their offspring succeed in life no matter what the situation is. Every parent does his or her best to see their child become a great personality. If they don't, we have to tell ourselves one thing: *«As long as my child has the breath of life, nothing is over yet.»* This breath of life should give you the assurance that everything is still possible, so don't give up. And don't let the present condition weaken you. The hardest thing nowadays is to see photos on social media of parents celebrating their children to do great things that you would have liked yours to do, such as playing football, running and other sports. Do not let this make you feel somehow, rejoice with them but also continue to water the seed in your child. As long as you are doing it well and with love, this will bring you great joy as well. Never compare your child to any other. I learned to love my child the way he is. This is why I am sharing our journey. To encourage as many parent possible not to give up on their loved ones.

I have to admit that despite everything, the most difficult thing for me was to accept my son's condition because I thought that a spell had been cast on him. Of course, this was a real drag for me for years. I wanted so much to see my child's condition changed overnight that I did not hesitate to try the impossible to achieve my goals. I went to strange

Conclusion

places and approached unsavoury people, because I believed that these places and people might have the solution I wanted. I travelled the four corners of the world to find the result that would make **Stephane** like other children and bring harmony to myself but these were useless. I regret nothing because it served to establish the truth that **God is the Solution to every situation** and time heals all wounds. But all that wasted time would have been used to give more love and attention to my son.

While I had not accepted my boy's condition did not had peace. Even in my family, the looks I received from few family and friends did not hide their contempt.

What I find intriguing when you have a disabled or with special need child is that people look at you accusingly or with pity.

«No, I don't want to be blamed because I have nothing to do with my son's condition. I don't want to be pitied either, it saddens me. Don't look at me and my son in a strange way because I don't like it. Why are you surprised that my son is disabled?»

«I don't want to be blamed me, I have not done anything wrong for my son to have this condition. I want you to have compassion because it comes with love and free from any negative feelings. Don't look at me and my son in a strange way because it break my heart. My son is able differently.»

After trying everything humanly possible to get my boy out of this condition, I realised that there are things that remain impossible to man no matter how much he wants them. Although I was already a Christian, I took a vow of faith again because my prayer life was at its lowest possible. I was weakened by everything I was going through. In truth, I thought that through this trial, God was inviting me to rejoin His ranks. So one night during a prayer, I said: *«Lord, maybe you are putting me through this trial because you need me to give you more attention, I accept to come back home...».*

Based on the book of **Matthew chapter 19 verse 26** which says: *«Jesus looked at them and said to them, 'This is impossible with men, but with God all things are possible.»* I prayed this prayer from the bottom of my heart: *«Lord, I have tried everything in my own strength, but I cannot obtain a favourable result for my son's condition. So, I come back to You and I ask Your forgiveness for everything. I place everything in Your hands, for I know that with You everything is possible. »*

I took a deep breath and surrendered EVERYTHING into the hands of the Lord. I decided to leave my worries, my pains, my unanswered questions, in the hands of my God and not to worry about them anymore. From that moment on, an immeasurable peace invaded my heart as if all preoccupations had henceforth fallen silent in the face of the power of the Most High. I, who had been worried, confused and agitated since **Stephane**'s birth, now felt relieved. The God of peace had indeed taken control and I could only concentrate on giving love to my children.

Now I can attest that after I joined Jesus Christ, my son **Stephane** has a better approach to the outside world. He is no longer that child for whom I had to plan everything, imagine everything, do everything. My little one has gone from being a difficult child to someone more gentle and open. I see life in him. It is true that he already existed, but this time it is different because Jesus Christ lives in him. These are not just words that I am writing to you one after the other, but an observation made by the mother that I am in the life of her child.

Conclusion

My son's condition, which was a source of shame, failure, sadness and even unhappiness in the past, has become a source of blessing.

If it wasn't for **Stephane**'s condition, the **Stephtogether** Foundation would not have been set up. This foundation is a source of support for children, parents and families who suffer not only from **autism, but** also from any other desperate and deprived condition.

I am amazed at the power of God when I hear my son praying to Him following the example set by Jesus Christ...

I no longer see my son as a separate person, but as the one through whom God has taught me to love despite the difference.

However, sometimes I am worried, but immediately I start to fervently declare: *«My son's situation is no longer in my hands but in the hands of God, the creator. He takes care of everything! »*

Maybe you have a child with **autism, Asperger's**, ADHD, Dyspraxia, Dyslexia or any learning difficulty   or in any other desperate and helpless condition, or any other disability, I would like to encourage you not to give up. Trust your creator. He may not change your child's condition, but by His power, the Lord will work to give you the peace, grace, strength and courage to continue on your journey. You will make it! Know that you are not alone, there are many of us and together we are stronger.

Despite the condition of your child, beloved, you are more than victorious. Look around you at how many people in this world seek to have just one child regardless of his condition. Then be a perfect parent. Do your part and let God do the rest. You didn't buy that child in the

Conclusion

market. If you did, you would have probably returned it to the seller and claim your money back. He is more precious in the eyes of God who created him than you who gave birth to him. Take courage my sister, take courage my brother. The fruit of your womb is blessed and one day, like me, you will tell your story in the past. Be strong and stay positive...

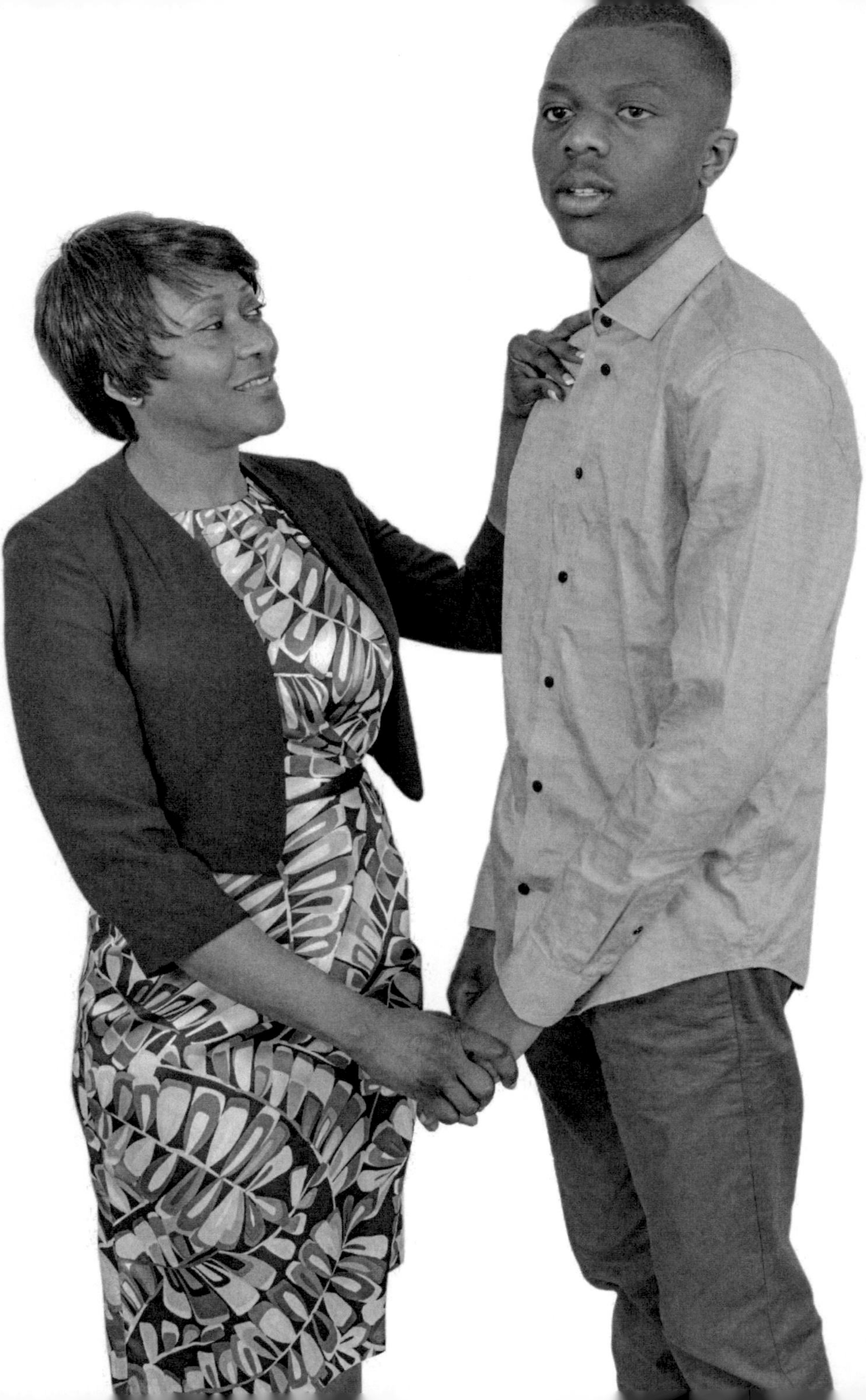

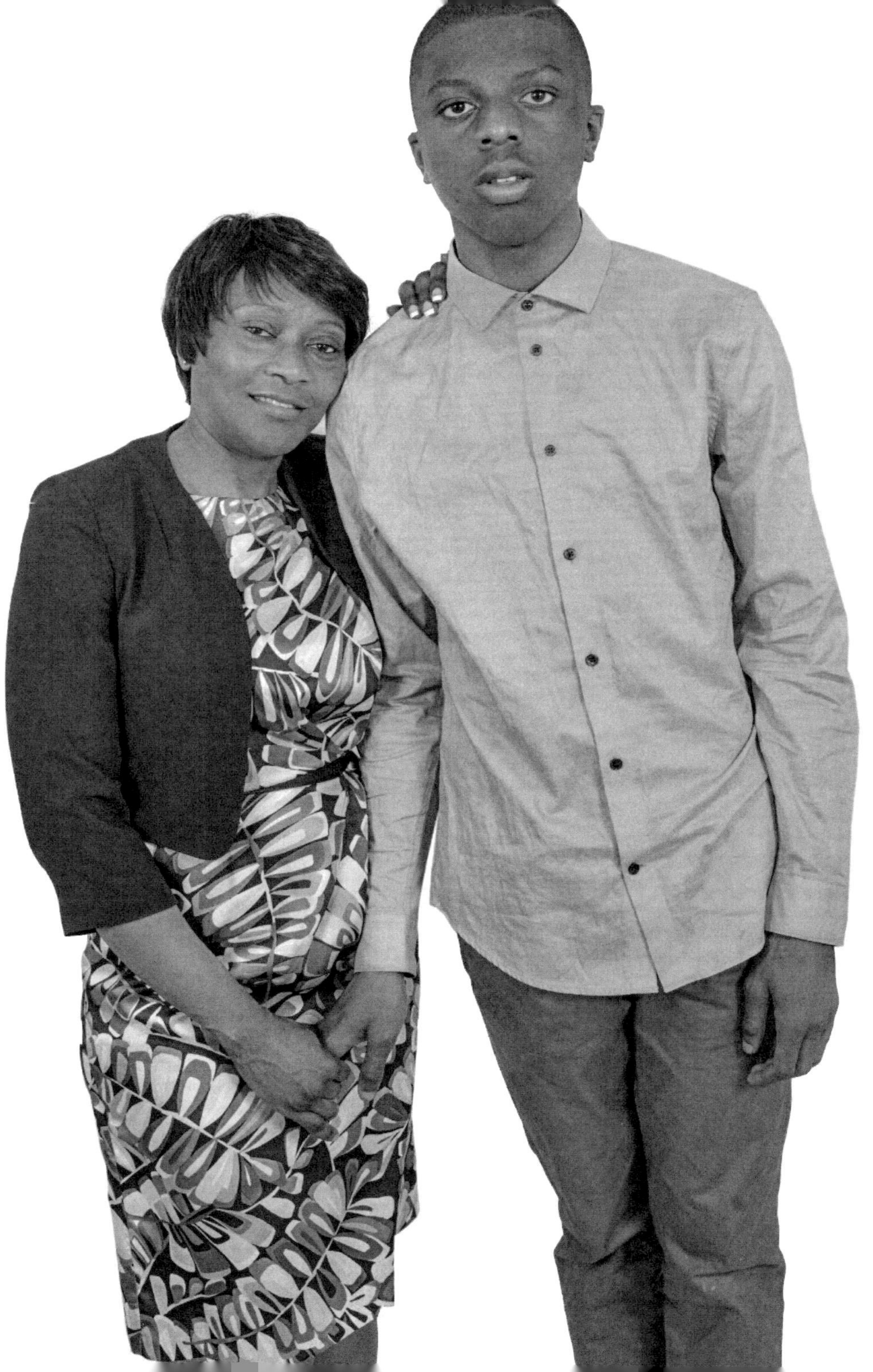